J
973.7349
Fitzgerald, Stephanie

Battle of Gettysburg

The Split History of the

BATTLE OF GETTYSBURG

UNION PERSPECTIVE

BY STEPHANIE FITZGERALD

CONTENT CONSULTANT:
Brett Barker, PhD
Associate Professor of History
University of Wisconsin–Marathon County

COMPASS POINT BOOKS
a capstone imprint

Compass Point Books are published by Capstone,
1710 Roe Crest Drive, North Mankato, Minnesota 56003
www.capstonepub.com

Library of Congress Cataloging-in-Publication Data
Fitzgerald, Stephanie.
  The split history of the Battle of Gettysburg : a perspectives flip book / by Stephanie Fitzgerald.
    pages cm.—(Perspectives flip books)
  Includes bibliographical references and index.
  Summary: "Describes the opposing viewpoints of the Union and the Confederacy during the Civil
War Battle of Gettysburg"—Provided by publisher.
  ISBN 978-0-7565-4695-3 (library binding)
  ISBN 978-0-7565-4701-1 (paperback)
  ISBN 978-0-7565-4703-5 (ebook PDF)
  ISBN 978-0-7565-4705-9 (reflowable epub)
1. Gettysburg, Battle of, Gettysburg, Pa., 1863—Juvenile literature. I. Title.
  E475.53.F574 2014
  973.7'349—dc23   2013007021

MANAGING EDITOR
CATHERINE NEITGE

LIBRARY CONSULTANT
KATHLEEN BAXTER

DESIGNERS
GENE BENTDAHL AND SARAH BENNETT

PRODUCTION SPECIALIST
LAURA MANTHE

MEDIA RESEARCHER
WANDA WINCH

IMAGE CREDITS

Union Perspective: CRIAimages.com: Jay Robert Nash Collection, 5, 16, 18; Library of Congress:
Prints and Photographs Division, 7, 14, 29, Alexander Gardner, 27, Edwin Forbes, 24–25, 26;
www. historicalimagebank.com, Painting by Don Troiani, cover (all), 11, 12, 20

Confederate Perspective: 20th Maine & 15th Alabama by Dale Gallon, Courtesy of Gallon
Historical Art, www.gallon.com, 19; Capstone, 9; CRIAimages.com: Jay Robert Nash Collection, 5,
12–13; Library of Congress: Prints and Photographs Division, 15, 18, 26–27, Edwin Forbes, 21, 29;
www. historicalimagebank.com, Painting by Don Troiani, cover (all), 7, 11, 24

Art elements: Shutterstock: Color Symphony, paper texture, Ebtikar, flag, Sandra Cunningham,
grunge photo, SvetlanaR, grunge lines

Printed in the United States of America in North Mankato, Minnesota.
032013   007223CGF13

0 1021 0280173 9

Table of Contents

THE ROAD TO GETTYSBURG

CH 1

In May 1863 morale was low in the camp of General

Joseph Hooker—and in the rest of the Union Army of the Potomac.

Hooker's men had just been badly beaten by the Confederate

Army at Chancellorsville, Virginia. By now, a war that most people

thought would be short had raged on for more than two years. Even

worse, the Union army was on a losing streak. Confederate General

Robert E. Lee's smaller, poorly equipped army kept winning

important battles. Many in the North worried that the Civil War

might soon be lost. They had reason to fear. The Confederates'

confidence was high, and General Lee was about to make a very

bold move.

President Lincoln (in top hat) reviewed the Union troops with General Hooker before the disastrous loss at Chancellorsville.

After losing 17,000 men in savage fighting at Chancellorsville, Hooker retreated to Falmouth, Virginia, on the north side of the Rappahannock River. His enemy, Lee's Army of Northern Virginia, was camped on the south side of the river in and near the town of Fredericksburg. Toward the end of the month, spies alerted Hooker that much of the southern army was on the move. The Confederates were preparing to march into Pennsylvania — Union territory.

When Hooker realized that Lee was moving his troops north, he proposed an attack on Richmond, Virginia, the Confederate capital. President Abraham Lincoln quickly denied the request. Lincoln urged Hooker to stay north of the Rappahannock River and not cross it. He wrote: "In one word, I would not take any risk of being entangled upon the river, like an ox jumped half over a fence and liable to be torn by dogs front and rear without a fair chance to gore one way or kick the other."

Several days later Lincoln wrote Hooker by telegram to follow Lee's army, keeping between it and the nation's capital of Washington, D.C. "Fight him when opportunity offers," Lincoln instructed.

On June 15 Confederate General Richard S. Ewell and his 2nd Corps defeated a Union garrison at Winchester, Virginia. The victory cleared the way for the Army of Northern Virginia to move through the Shenandoah Valley toward Pennsylvania. When word of the defeat reached Hooker, he started shifting his troops northward to keep the Army of the Potomac between Washington, D.C., and Lee's army.

MEADE TAKES CHARGE

By June 26 Hooker's army was on its way to Frederick, Maryland. He asked for reinforcements from his commanders in Washington. When his request was denied, Hooker offered his resignation. President Abraham Lincoln, who was eager to be rid of the ineffective general, accepted. He handed command to General George Meade, who was certain a battle was coming. Meade continued pushing the men north and ordered his cavalry to confront the Confederates.

Two brigades led by General John Buford rode into Gettysburg, Pennsylvania, on June 30. Buford learned that a large column of Confederate troops had passed through town a few days before. He

General George Meade (seated, third from left) and fellow generals in the Army of the Potomac

also found out that as many as 20,000 more were located in Cashtown, 8 miles (13 kilometers) to the west, and headed toward Gettysburg.

Buford quickly realized that the town—and his 2,800 troops—lay between two very large parts of the Army of Northern Virginia. Buford sent a courier to General John Reynolds, whose 1st Corps was camped 6 miles (9.7 km) to the southwest. Then Buford organized his troops in a defensive position along the ridges to the west of town. He knew it was important to take and hold the high ground. It is easier to defend a high elevation than it is to climb and take it.

In the two days since he'd been named commander of the Army of the Potomac, Meade had devised a strategy. It did not include a battle in Gettysburg. He had planned to lure Lee into attacking his forces in Maryland. Now Meade reluctantly changed his plans and ordered his army north to Pennsylvania. He gave command of the 3rd and 11th corps to Reynolds and ordered him to lead those corps, along with his 1st, in support of Buford. Almost by accident, the path to the greatest battle of the Civil War had been set.

A NATION DIVIDED

The Civil War tore the United States apart and cost hundreds of thousands of lives. It lasted four years, from 1861 to 1865, and killed more than 620,000 soldiers. Another 100,000 civilians died in the bloody conflict. The war pitted the northern Union against the southern Confederacy. The South, which based its economy on slave labor, wanted to keep the institution of slavery as well as expand it into other states and territories. Most northerners wanted to halt its spread or end it all together. With the 1860 election of Republican Abraham Lincoln as president, antislavery forces ruled the nation. Southern states began to leave the Union. South Carolina led the way, seceding in December 1860. In the early months of 1861, other states joined South Carolina to form the Confederacy: Alabama, Florida, Georgia, Louisiana, Mississippi, and Texas. On April 12, 1861, Confederate soldiers fired on Fort Sumter in South Carolina, beginning the Civil War. Within a week Virginia began the process to secede. Arkansas, North Carolina, and Tennessee followed.

DAY ONE:

TERRIBLE CASUALTIES

*T*he first Confederates to approach Gettysburg a little

after sunrise on the morning of July 1 were in a division under

General Henry Heth. They came from Cashtown, heading for town

on a road called the Chambersburg Pike.

One of Heth's brigades, under Joseph Davis, was deployed

north of the pike. Another, led by James Archer, was deployed

to the south. Buford watched as Heth's brigades attacked his

cavalrymen about 7:30 a.m. Buford was behind the lines high up on

Seminary Ridge, just east of McPherson's Ridge. He realized his thin line of cavalry would not be able to hold out for long against the Confederates. About 10 a.m. General Reynolds arrived.

Reynolds sent aides riding south to hurry his men along. He ordered a division under General James Wadsworth to leave the road and cut across the fields outside of Gettysburg to get to the fight quicker.

One of Wadsworth's brigades, led by General Lysander Cutler, came toward McPherson's Ridge north of the Chambersburg Pike. Just as the exhausted Union cavalry was about to give way, Cutler's men took up the fight.

A GENERAL FALLS

The other half of Wadsworth's division, the Iron Brigade, was moving south of the pike to attack the Confederates through a small patch of woods on the top of the ridge. As Reynolds turned in his saddle to urge his men into the fight, he was struck by a minie ball, a cone-shaped bullet. Just as the battle was beginning, the general fell dead from his horse.

Reynolds' orderly, Charles A. Veil, later described his commander's death in a letter. He wrote, in part, "He never spoke a word, or moved, a muscle after he was struck. I have seen many men killed in action, but never saw a ball do its work so instantly as did the ball which struck General Reynolds, a man who knew not what fear or danger was, in a word, was one of our very best Generals."

Meanwhile, Cutler's brigade was in trouble. Davis' troops were ready when the Union soldiers appeared. The close-range fighting

The men of the Iron Brigade lost their beloved general, John Reynolds, early in the fighting.

resulted in terrible casualties on both sides. As Cutler's men began to fall back, the northern part of the Union line bent back east.

The 6th Wisconsin regiment stopped along the road and fired at Davis' soldiers. Many of Davis' men took cover in an unfinished railroad cut that ran parallel to the Chambersburg Pike. The trench had been dug for a railroad line. With its high sides, the cut seemed to offer perfect cover for the Confederates. However, the railroad cut got deeper as it ran east. At that point, the walls of the ditch were about 15 feet (4.6 meters) high—too high for the Confederates to shoot over. When Cutler's men realized what was happening, they charged forward to trap the Confederates. Two hundred of Davis' men surrendered to the Union troops.

The battle died down a little after 11 a.m., as both sides regrouped. Major General Oliver Howard arrived in Gettysburg leading his 11th Corps. He took command of the Union forces.

A soldier in the 6th Wisconsin regiment fought to grab the Confederate flag.

He used two divisions to extend the Union line north and east of Gettysburg. A third division was placed in reserve on Cemetery Hill, an elevated spot just south of town.

Howard then passed command of the 11th Corps to General Carl Schurz, who was ordered to form an east-to-west line north of town using three divisions. The left flank would meet up with the flank of the 1st Corps still on McPherson's Ridge.

But the 11th's right flank—commanded by Brigadier General Francis Barlow—was unprotected. The men soon came under heavy fire. Barlow was wounded as he tried to rally the crumbling Union line. His men began to panic.

By 4:30 p.m. both the 1st and 11th corps were retreating through the town of Gettysburg to the fortified position on Cemetery Hill. "On every side our troops were madly rushing to the rear," recalled a Wisconsin volunteer. "My heart sank within me. I lost all hope."

A HELPING HAND

Brigadier General Francis Barlow's own Union troops were unable to help their wounded leader during the battle. But he was later found by Confederate soldiers who moved him to what they thought was a safe spot and shared their water with him. Confederate doctors tended to his wounds. When Confederate troops left Gettysburg they were unable to take Barlow or their own severely wounded soldiers with them. Barlow was left behind and not taken prisoner. Although he was seriously wounded, Barlow later recovered and returned to duty.

OCCUPY THE HILLS

Then Major General Winfield Scott Hancock, commander of the 2nd Corps, arrived on the field. Meade had ordered him to assess the situation at Gettysburg and take command if Reynolds was injured or killed.

Hancock realized that the troops on Cemetery Hill faced a threat from Culp's Hill, about a half mile (805 meters) southeast of their position. If the Confederates took Culp's Hill, which was higher than Cemetery Hill, they would be able to force the Union troops to abandon their location. Hancock ordered Wadsworth to take what was left of his division to occupy Culp's Hill.

Hancock was right about the southern army's goal. But by the time the Confederate troops advanced to what they thought was an unoccupied position, they were met by concentrated fire from Wadsworth's men. The Union soldiers had been on the hill for more

A 1913 map showcased the battlefield 50 years after the momentous events.

than an hour—plenty of time to build strong fortifications made of logs and rocks. The Confederates returned to camp for the night.

General Meade arrived in Gettysburg before dawn on July 2 and surveyed the scene from Cemetery Hill. He could see that Hancock's men were in a strong position. The Union line started at the top of Culp's Hill, ran west to Cemetery Hill, and then turned sharply south and ran in a straight line to Little Round Top. The Union held the high ground.

Meade's objective now was to gather his army and hold the position. During the fighting the 1st and 11th corps had been reinforced by Major General Henry Slocum's 12th Corps and most of the 3rd Corps under General Daniel Sickles. But many of the Union's troops were still marching toward Gettysburg.

DAY TWO:

ATTACK AND COUNTERATTACK

By the morning of July 2, 83,000 Union troops were ready to face about 75,000 Confederates. Many of the men had marched all night to reach Gettysburg. Most were too tired and footsore to pitch their tents when they arrived. But by sunrise the exhausted soldiers were on the front line.

The Union troops were set out in General Meade's "fishhook" line along Cemetery Ridge—a long line that curved at the end like a fishhook. The line curved and ended at Culp's Hill on the north. For the moment, the northern soldiers held the high ground.

SICKLES' FOLLY

When General Sickles arrived at Cemetery Ridge that morning, Meade placed him and his 3rd Corps in line, facing west, south of Hancock's 2nd Corps. Sickles was not pleased. The Cemetery Hill elevation dropped off by the time it got to Sickles' line. Although Little Round Top flanked the position, the general didn't think he had enough men to stretch the line far enough to occupy that hill. In front of him was mostly bare ground broken only by a small peach orchard.

Confederate guns shell Union soldiers at Cemetery Ridge.

Sickles wanted to move his men west to occupy the rise around the Peach Orchard, as the battlefield came to be called. Meade said no. Meade wanted an unbroken line of defense along Cemetery Ridge. Sickles' men would have to remain in place.

Upset, Sickles took matters into his own hands. He moved his corps into position facing west along the Emmitsburg Road and running south to the Peach Orchard. At the orchard, the line turned sharply east and ran through a forest to Houck's Ridge just west of Little Round Top. It ended at a place the soldiers named Devil's Den—a field littered with boulders and large rocks. Sickles' men were now cut off from the rest of the Union line and sticking out almost a mile (1.6 km) in a vulnerable, thinly stretched line.

At 4 p.m., when Meade rode out to inspect the troops, he was horrified to find Sickles gone from his original position. He rode out to the Peach Orchard to confront the general. He arrived just in time for the start of the Confederate attack.

Meade sent one of Hancock's divisions in to reinforce Sickles' men. The Union troops were pushed out of the Peach Orchard, a battlefield called the Wheat Field, and into the Devil's Den. As the Union soldiers fought desperately to hold on, Meade sent in more reinforcements—this time the 5th Corps under General George Sykes.

The fresh soldiers would be of great help to the men in Devil's Den. But their deployment severely weakened the rest of the battle line. Confederate troops were now moving steadily toward an important position—Little Round Top. If they took it, the Union army would face destruction and a Confederate victory.

Union troops rush to reinforce their fellow soldiers.

LITTLE ROUND TOP

After discovering that Sickles had moved his line, Meade had sent his chief engineer, Major General Gouverneur Warren, to make sure Little Round Top had not been left undefended. There was only a small signal team stationed on the hill. The team's job was to notify the Union generals of the enemy's movements.

As Warren watched, he saw Confederate troops on the move. He realized that the Union line was about to be surrounded—and that Little Round Top was the only defensive position that might save it. Warren set out at a gallop with a desperate call for reinforcements.

Warren quickly came upon one unit of Sykes' brigade. He sent them to defend the hill. The soldiers had barely arrived and started organizing their line when Confederate soldiers swarmed the Union regiments on the southwest slope. The men were able to fight off the first attack, but crumbled under a second assault. Just when it seemed all might be lost, help arrived in the form of the 140th New York, which was able to beat back the Confederate charge.

The 20th Maine regiment held the southeast slope of Little Round Top. Colonel Joshua Lawrence Chamberlain was the regiment's leader. The soldiers' position meant that they held the left flank of the entire Union Army of the Potomac. If they couldn't hold, the way would be clear for a Union defeat.

Twice, Alabama soldiers surged up the hill. Twice, the 20th beat them back. At this point many of the Maine soldiers were out of ammunition. Desperate, they dug through their dead and wounded comrades' possessions for more. Once again the Confederates surged, and the Union line began to crumble. Chamberlain ordered his men to fix their bayonets and charge the enemy. The Alabamans were stunned by the attack. Many fled. Others threw down their weapons and surrendered.

Little Round Top had been saved, but Sickles' men in the Devil's Den were doomed. The 3rd Corps, along with those who had been sent to reinforce them, had finally been pushed back. The survivors beat a hasty retreat to Cemetery Ridge.

HOLDING THE CENTER

Meanwhile, the center of the Union line—from Big and Little Round Top to Hancock's position on the upper end of Cemetery Ridge—had completely fallen apart. Hancock looked for reinforcements to fill the gap. As a 1,500-man brigade from Alabama headed for his position, Hancock found the 262 men of the 1st Minnesota. Without a moment's hesitation, the soldiers charged across the open field to confront an enemy with five times as many men.

William Lochren of the 1st Minnesota later wrote, "Every man realized in an instant what that order meant—death or wounds to us all; the sacrifice of the regiment to gain a few minutes' time and save the position, and probably the battlefield."

The greatly outnumbered 1st Minnesota volunteers charge the enemy.

The shocked Alabamans stopped their advance momentarily. They quickly regrouped, however, and rained bullets upon the Minnesotans. Only 47 of the men of the 1st Minnesota made it out of the charge unharmed.

"Reinforcements were coming on the run, but I knew that before they could reach the threatened point the Confederates, unless checked, would seize the position," Hancock wrote later. "I would have ordered that regiment in if I had known that every man would be killed. It had to be done."

But the 1st Minnesota's heroic effort didn't stop the Confederates. A brigade under Confederate General Ambrose Wright was on the verge of cutting the Union line on Cemetery Ridge in two. But the Union troops refused to yield. With night falling and nearly 700 casualties, Wright pulled back.

Though the line on Cemetery Ridge had held, the Union army was still under threat at Culp's Hill. Most of the soldiers of the 12th Corps under General Slocum were ordered to leave their position to reinforce Sickles. Now just one brigade held the hill. Shortly after 8 p.m., General Richard Ewell's Confederate troops launched their attack.

A line of artillery just below the cemetery gate had been blasting the Confederates all day. Now the southern troops were advancing, somehow managing to push the northern infantry all the way back to the guns. The men fought among the cannons with bayonets and fists—sometimes using their muskets as clubs—until the Union troops finally retreated through the cemetery.

Then came a counterattack by the Union 11th Corps. With darkness—and more Union soldiers—coming on quickly, the Confederates abandoned the hill.

At Culp's Hill the Confederate line held a position halfway up the hill as darkness fell. The Union troops could expect a renewed attack in the morning.

That evening General Meade held a conference with his corps commanders. Lee had attacked both the Union's flanks and failed. There was only one goal left. Meade told his men to prepare for an attack on their center.

CIVILIAN DEATH

Mary Virginia Wade was the only civilian to be killed during the three-day battle at Gettysburg. The 20-year-old woman known as Jennie was staying at her sister's house, located in the middle of the fighting. Many bullets and artillery shells hit the home during the battle. One struck Jennie as she stood in the kitchen baking bread for the Union soldiers. She was killed instantly.

CH. 4 DAY THREE: FINAL SHOWDOWN

General Meade was sure the main Confederate assault would come at his center. But the southern soldiers on Culp's Hill also posed a threat. At 4 a.m. the 12th Corps, led by General Alpheus Williams, began the work of driving them out.

Williams gathered all the artillery he could and unleashed a barrage on the southern soldiers gathered below. As the Confederates charged up the hill, they were showered with cannon fire, as well as bullets from infantrymen positioned behind walls.

As mounds of dead and wounded southern troops piled up in front of the Union position, the Confederates finally pulled back.

At 1 p.m. Confederate artillery unleashed a massive attack, firing about 150 cannons at the center of the Union line. But the aim was not always on target. Rather than falling among the infantry, much of the fire was flying beyond the lines. It hit the soldiers who occupied the back slope of Cemetery Ridge.

CANNON FIRE

The Union artillery responded almost immediately. About 80 guns spewed fire at the Confederate gunners exposed in the field below. The aim of the Union guns was also imperfect. But by overshooting their targets, the Union gunners were hitting the southern infantry waiting to assault their line. The Confederates suffered hundreds of casualties before even launching their attack.

Newspaper artist Edwin Forbes captured the fierce fighting on Culp's Hill.

After almost two hours, the Union guns fell silent. Officers realized that they needed to save ammunition for the coming assault. As Union soldiers peered through the smoke covering the field before them, about 12,500 Confederate soldiers stepped out from the trees along the east side of Seminary Ridge.

The Union soldiers were told to hold their fire until the enemy got close. "We could not help hitting them at every shot," an officer recalled.

CEMETERY HILL

Cemetery Hill got its name from Evergreen Cemetery, which was located at its crest. Ironically, a sign posted on the entrance to the cemetery read: "All persons found using firearms in these grounds will be prosecuted with the utmost rigor of the law."

Edwin Forbes, a staff artist for Frank Leslie's Illustrated Newspaper, *witnessed the Confederates' unsuccessful attempt to break the Union line.*

But the Confederates kept coming. Union infantry were positioned behind a low stone wall that extended beyond either side of a group of trees. The Union soldiers opened fire as soon as the Confederates came into view. Cannons shot canisters of ammunition. As each canister exploded, it sent dozens of small metal balls through the ranks of Confederate soldiers.

The southerners were pushed back, but soon surged forward again. As they closed on the wall, the northerners began to fall back. The Army of the Potomac was taking heavy casualties, but it was inflicting many more. The Confederate attack was finally beaten back. The southerners retreated to Seminary Ridge.

Many officers urged Meade to attack the broken and battered Army of Northern Virginia at Seminary Ridge. They were sure they could end the war that day. But Meade chose caution. He feared that if he sent his men across that open field, they would suffer the same fate that had just befallen the Confederates. And, as he made clear in a letter he had read to the troops, his greatest concern was pushing and keeping the Confederates out of northern territory — not destroying them. He wrote, "The commanding general looks to the army for greater efforts to drive from our soil every vestige of the presence of the invader."

Dead Confederate soldiers await burial after the Battle of Gettysburg.

President Lincoln was appalled when he heard Meade's words. He wanted the Confederates brought to their knees. He exclaimed, "Drive the invaders from our soil. My God! Is that all? Will our generals never get that idea out of their heads? The whole country is our soil!"

The Army of the Potomac had survived the bloodiest battle of the Civil War. They'd suffered 23,000 casualties but had stopped Lee's invasion of the North.

NEW BIRTH OF FREEDOM

By July 4 the battle of Gettysburg was over. The summer sun beat down on the bodies of wounded and dead men and animals. Both armies spent the day gathering their wounded. Soldiers, prisoners, and townspeople buried many of the dead in shallow graves.

Eventually the bodies of the Union soldiers would be dug up and reburied in a cemetery created in their honor. When the cemetery was dedicated November 19, 1863, President Lincoln gave a short speech, one of the most famous ever written. He ended his Gettysburg Address by saying:

"We here highly resolve that these dead shall not have died in vain, that this nation under God shall have a new birth of freedom, and that government of the people, by the people, for the people shall not perish from the earth."

The Confederate army would never attempt to invade the North again. But the Civil War would drag on for almost two more years before ending with a Union victory. The United States of America had been bloodied and battered, but—as Lincoln had resolved—it had not perished from the earth.

Four months after the battle, President Lincoln (bareheaded, in the center) delivered his most famous speech at the dedication of the Gettysburg National Cemetery.

INDEX

COMPASS POINT BOOKS
a capstone imprint

CONTENT CONSULTANT:
Brett Barker, PhD
Associate Professor of History
University of Wisconsin—Marathon County

BY STEPHANIE FITZGERALD

CONFEDERATE PERSPECTIVE

BATTLE OF GETTYSBURG

The Split History of the

A PERSPECTIVES FLIP BOOK

About the Author:

Stephanie Fitzgerald is the author of many nonfiction books for children. She especially enjoys writing about history and wildlife. Stephanie lives in Stamford, Connecticut, with her husband, Brian, and her daughter, Molly.

Source Notes:

Union Perspective
Page 5, line 12: Richard Wheeler. *Gettysburg 1863: Campaign of Endless Echoes*. New York: Plume, 1999, p. 40.
Page 6, line 5: James McPherson. *Battle Cry of Freedom: The Civil War Era*. New York: Oxford University Press, 2003, p. 651.
Page 10, line 19: National Park Civil War Series: The Battle of Gettysburg. July 1—the Battle Opens. 21 May 2013. http://www.nps.gov/history/history/online_books/civil_war_series/16/sec3.htm
Page 12, line 14: *Voices of the Civil War: Gettysburg*. Alexandria, Va.: Time-Life Books, 1995, p. 38.
Page 20, line 8: Brian Leehan. *Pale Horse at Plum Run: The First Minnesota at Gettysburg*. St. Paul: Minnesota Historical Society Press, 2002, pp. 56–57.
Page 21, line 5: Ibid., p. 57.
Page 25, line 7: Geoffrey C. Ward. *The Civil War: An Illustrated History*. New York: Knopf, 1990, p. 232.
Page 25, sidebar, line 3: Ibid., p. 216.
Page 27, line 6: *Gettysburg 1863: Campaign of Endless Echoes*, p. 278.
Page 28, line 3: Wilmer L. Jones. *Generals in Blue and Gray: Vol. 1, Lincoln's Generals*. Mechanicsburg, Pa.: Stackpole Books, 2006, p. 294.
Page 28, line 19: Transcription of Gettysburg Address from the Lincoln Memorial. 21 May 2013. http://myloc.gov/Exhibitions/gettysburgaddress/exhibitionitems/Pages/MemorialTranscription.html

Confederate Perspective:
Page 5, line 1: *The Civil War: An Illustrated History*, p. 10.
Page 6, sidebar, line 6: Ibid., p. 12.
Page 9, line 4: Eric J. Wittenberg. *The Battle of Brandy Station: North America's Largest Cavalry Battle*. Charleston, S.C.: The History Press, 2010, pp. 49–50.
Page 12, line 4: *Voices of the Civil War: Gettysburg*, p. 42.
Page 16, line 10: *Gettysburg 1863: Campaign of Endless Echoes*, p. 191.
Page 16, line 17: Bruce Catton. *Gettysburg: The Final Fury*. Garden City, N.Y.: Doubleday, 1974, p. 36.
Page 20, line 1: *The Civil War: An Illustrated History*, p. 221.
Page 25, line 19: *Gettysburg 1863: Campaign of Endless Echoes*, p. 252.
Page 28, line 1: *Battle Cry of Freedom: The Civil War Era*, p. 663.

Table of Contents

BEFORE THE BATTLE

By May of 1863, the Civil War between the United States of America and the Confederate States of America had been raging for more than two years. The fighting had ravaged much of the southern countryside.

But the people of the Confederacy thought they had every chance of winning the war. The Union army had more men, more supplies, and better equipment than General Robert E. Lee's Army of Northern Virginia. But the general had recently pulled off victories in several major battles—Fredericksburg, Second Manassas, and Chancellorsville.

The Battle of Chancellorsville became known as "Lee's perfect battle."

"Nothing gave me much concern so long as I knew that Gen. Lee was in command," said artillery Colonel E. Porter Alexander later. "We looked forward to victory under him as confidently as to successive sunrises."

A DARING PLAN

As his troops rested in Fredericksburg, Virginia, Lee proposed to follow his success at Chancellorsville with an invasion of southern Pennsylvania in Union territory. He believed that if he attacked the cities of Harrisburg and Philadelphia, it would throw the Union into a panic. It would force the Army of the Potomac to chase Lee's army through Maryland and Pennsylvania in an effort to defend Washington, D.C., the nation's capital. If Lee could capture the Union capital, his army stood a good chance of winning the war.

A northern invasion would also solve one of the Confederate army's biggest problems. Much of the fighting had taken place on southern soil. Crops and livestock were depleted to the point that there was little to feed the citizens, let alone the army. If Lee could lead his troops into the rich farmlands of southern Pennsylvania, they would finally have plenty of food, as well as other supplies—such as shoes and clothing—that they could buy from the local people.

Lee organized his 70,000 infantrymen into three corps for the invasion: The 1st Corps, led by General James Longstreet, the 2nd, led by General Richard S. Ewell, and the 3rd under General A. P. Hill. Lieutenant General James Ewell Brown "Jeb" Stuart commanded Lee's cavalry, which consisted of 10,000 horsemen.

JUST PUNISHMENT

General Robert E. Lee had issued orders to keep his men from stealing from the people of Pennsylvania. They were to pay—in nearly worthless Confederate money—for anything they took. But his orders were often ignored. "The rascals are afraid we are going to overrun Pennsylvania," said Colonel Clement Evans of the 31st Georgia. "That would indeed be glorious, if we could ravage that state making her desolate like Virginia. It would be a just punishment."

Generals Lee (on white horse) and Stuart review the cavalry at Brandy Station.

The cavalry had been crucial to Lee's victories. Stuart and his men provided quick and accurate information about the enemy's movements and positions. This had helped Lee consistently outsmart his opponents.

By June 5 the cavalry was encamped at Brandy Station, Virginia. While he waited for the rest of the army to arrive, Stuart decided to throw a party. It would include a review of his troops by important civilians in the area. He held a second review when Lee arrived June 8. The general moved on almost immediately after.

About 4:30 a.m. June 9, Union cavalry surprised Stuart's troops as they slept. The battle lasted 12 hours, until the Union troops finally retreated. They had fought well and had shown the southerners that they would now face a more equal opponent on horseback. The Confederates could claim victory, but they had lost something important. The Union army now knew that Lee was on the move. They just weren't sure where he was going. Stuart suffered a loss, as well—a blow to his pride that would result in a major error.

THE MARCH NORTH

Meanwhile, the rest of the Confederate army continued its advance. Ewell's corps attacked a Union garrison at Winchester on June 13. Within two days they wiped out the last Union obstacle between them and the Potomac River.

The Confederate and Union cavalries continued to clash, but the southern horsemen were able to screen the movements of their infantry. The Army of Northern Virginia continued to move undetected toward Pennsylvania.

As the rest of the army crossed the Potomac into Maryland, Stuart asked for permission to take three of his best brigades on a raid. He was still smarting from his embarrassment at Brandy Station and wanted revenge.

Stuart set out to ride around the Union army on June 25. He hoped to disrupt their supply lines and cut off their communication. Lee gave Stuart permission to go as long as he made sure to get back in time to screen the Army of Northern Virginia's advance

into Pennsylvania. But neither man realized that the Union Army was also on the move. Stuart would end up delayed for a week. Lee was marching toward one of the most important battles of the war without what he called his "eyes and ears."

Lee was in Chambersburg, Pennsylvania, on June 28. The rest of his army was spread out to the north, south, and east. Without information from Stuart, he had no idea where the Union troops were—until a spy entered camp. He informed a shocked Lee that the entire Army of the Potomac had gathered near Frederick, Maryland. If the northerners came upon any of Lee's strung-out forces, the Army of Northern Virginia could be destroyed. Lee quickly sent a message to General Richard Ewell, who spread the word to his commanders. The troops were to gather near Gettysburg. Twelve roads met there. Lee's men could follow those roads and all meet up in the middle.

Thousands of soldiers marched to Gettysburg.

FIRST DAY:

CAUGHT IN THE CUT

A scouting party led by General Jubal Early had first arrived in Gettysburg on June 26. They had gathered supplies and moved on. Four days later Brigadier General James Johnston Pettigrew was sent to look for any supplies Early might have missed. What he discovered instead was Union cavalry. He quickly reported back to his commander, General Henry Heth. The general was not pleased that his men had been chased off by what he assumed were local militia.

General John Buford leads his Union cavalry near McPherson's Ridge.

In the early morning hours of July 1, Heth led his division toward Gettysburg on a road called the Chambersburg Pike. As he approached McPherson's Ridge just west of town, Heth quickly realized he was not dealing with local volunteers. He was facing a line of 2,800 Union cavalry troops under the command of General John Buford.

Heth deployed two brigades on either side of the road. Joseph Davis led one brigade and James Archer led the other. The two brigades were near Herr's Ridge, 2 miles (3.2 km) west of Gettysburg, when they met Buford's men. The Union troops surrounded Archer's men and forced them to flee or surrender.

Davis' men had better luck—at first. Three regiments of Union soldiers charged across an open field to challenge the Confederates. The two sides blasted at each other at close range until the northerners fell back.

FIERCE FIGHTING

The Confederate troops discovered a cut that ran parallel to the Chambersburg Pike. It was a trench that had been dug for an unfinished railroad line. The cut provided great cover for the men who hopped inside. "I think there never was such slaughter as we made on this occasion," recalled Private Andrew Park of the 42nd Mississippi. "I could have walked a half or three quarters of a mile on the dead soldiers of the enemy and not have put my feet on the ground. In some places they were lying three deep."

But Union reinforcements soon arrived along the eastern end of the trench. As the cut moved east, it deepened to about 15 feet (4.6 meters). Before long Union troops surrounded the Confederates. The walls of the cut were too steep for the southerners to shoot over or climb over. Davis' men were forced to surrender.

General A.P. Hill's Confederate division attacks Union soldiers, pushing them back.

Quiet settled over the field as both sides waited for reinforcements. As the Union set up a defensive line north of town and placed reserves on Cemetery Hill, Ewell's 2nd Corps was approaching.

General Robert Rodes' troops were the first division of Ewell's corps to reach the scene. They gathered on Oak Hill, where Rodes saw an opportunity to attack the right flank of the Union line on McPherson's Ridge.

Meanwhile, Jubal Early's wing of Ewell's corps had also arrived in Gettysburg and found itself in the perfect position to attack the Union's 11th Corps. By that time Lee had arrived in Gettysburg and learned of Ewell's attack. As Early's men crashed into the northerners, Lee ordered Hill—who had been held back in reserve—to join the fight as well.

Rodes' men continued to press their attack while fresh troops lent their strength to the assault on McPherson's Ridge. Pettigrew's regiments fought a desperate battle with the Union soldiers. After many casualties were suffered on both sides, the Union line began to crumble. The Union 1st and 11th corps were on the run. The Confederates chased them through the town of Gettysburg to their fortified position on Cemetery Hill.

As the fighting in Gettysburg's streets died down, Lee sent a message to Ewell. He told the general to continue the assault and attack Cemetery Hill if he thought it could be taken. Ewell didn't think it could. The Army of Northern Virginia was not yet at full strength—more troops were still en route to Gettysburg. And the northerners held a strong position on the high ground. Instead Ewell set his sights on Culp's Hill, 1 mile (1.6 km) southeast of Cemetery Hill. Culp's Hill was even higher than Cemetery Hill.

WALKING WOUNDED

Many soldiers in the Civil War continued fighting even after receiving terrible wounds. General Richard Ewell had been wounded at the Second Battle of Manassas and lost a leg. But that didn't stop him from fighting. He returned to duty wearing a wooden leg, just in time for the Gettysburg campaign. While his troops were on the march, Ewell rode along in a buggy. At the onset of fighting, his aides would strap him to his horse's saddle.

Union soldiers lie dead on the Gettysburg battlefield.

But Ewell wasn't able to quickly organize his battle-weary soldiers. By the time he was ready to attack, at around 6 p.m., Union forces had already occupied Culp's Hill. The Confederates retired to their camp for the night.

THE ENEMY IS THERE

General James Longstreet arrived ahead of his troops after the fighting July 1. He joined Lee on Seminary Ridge as his commander watched the last of the routed Union soldiers climb Cemetery Hill.

Lee was encouraged by his army's success on the first day of fighting—and soon his army would be at close to full strength. He planned to renew the attack the next day. But Longstreet argued for a different approach.

If they followed Lee's plan, Longstreet said, they would have to send their men across open ground against a powerful enemy. The losses would be tremendous. It would make more sense, he argued, for the Army of Northern Virginia to move around the Union soldiers and get between them and Washington, D.C.

"The Federals will be sure to attack us," he explained. "When they attack we shall beat them … and the probabilities are that the fruits of our success will be great."

But Lee could not risk moving his army without knowing the full strength and position of the Union troops. Jeb Stuart still had not returned from his raiding mission. Without Stuart's report, Lee could not be sure what he would run into if he tried to move his entire army around the Union lines. "No," he told Longstreet. "The enemy is there and I am going to fight him there."

SECOND DAY:

SCALING THE HEIGHTS

*A*s dawn broke July 2, Lee's enemy held a strong position.

Union General Meade had deployed his line in what became known as

a "fishhook" formation. The 12th Corps on Culp's Hill joined up with

parts of the 1st and 11th corps along Cemetery Hill. Next came the

2nd Corps, which stretched down Cemetery Ridge. They joined with

the 3rd Corps, which ran to the southern edge of Cemetery Ridge.

Lee's three corps lined up across from the Union soldiers.

General Hill's men were on Seminary Ridge — the Confederate's

center — facing the 1st and 11th Union corps on Cemetery Hill.

The Slaughter Pen, part of the battlefield near Little Round Top, was covered with the dead.

Ewell's line started on Hill's left and ran east, passing Cemetery Hill and curving around Culp's Hill. Longstreet, whose men were not yet in position, would make up the right flank.

When Longstreet got into position, he was surprised to find that the Union 3rd Corps under General Daniel Sickles had moved out of position. Sickles' troops, now separated from the rest of the Union soldiers, were stretched out in a line that stuck out toward the Confederate position. At 4 p.m. Longstreet ordered his attack. Sickles' line broke, and the men ran. But Union reinforcements soon arrived. The casualties mounted as infantrymen fought their way through battlefields known as the Wheat Field, the Devil's Den, and the Valley of Death.

Late that afternoon General Jeb Stuart and his cavalry finally arrived, too late to play a significant role in the battle. Lee was not pleased with his cavalry commander.

As fighting raged on, the 15th Alabama under Colonel William C. Oates scrambled up Big Round Top. Oates saw that Little Round Top—to the northeast—was basically undefended. He realized that if he could get his guns to the summit, directly overlooking the Union lines, he could attack them. He hurried his men to their goal. But they arrived 10 minutes too late.

While Oates was rallying his men, the Union's chief engineer Major General Gouverneur Warren had arranged the defense of Little Round Top. The Alabamans fought desperately to take the hill. The Union soldiers finally fixed their bayonets and charged. Startled, the Confederates turned and ran, only to be faced with Union guns shooting at them from the opposite direction.

Colonel William Oates and the 15th Alabama attempt to take Little Round Top.

"While one man was shot in the face, his right-hand or left-hand comrade was shot in the side or back," Oates remembered. "Some were struck simultaneously [with] two or three balls from different directions."

As General Meade sent more Union forces to reinforce Sickles, he left gaps in his line. The Confederates were quick to take advantage of them.

At the center of the Union line, an Alabama brigade fought a desperate battle with the 1st Minnesota regiment. More than two-thirds of the Union troops fell, but they refused to give up their position.

More Confederate troops surged into the fight. General Ambrose Wright's brigade broke through the Union line briefly, but the Union soldiers managed to close the line again. As night was falling, Wright gave up the attack.

ATTACK THE HILL

The Army of Northern Virginia was having better luck elsewhere on the field. Ewell was focusing his men on Culp's Hill. That Union position had also been weakened when reinforcements were needed on the field. Around 8 p.m. Ewell sent three brigades to attack the Union brigade positioned there.

Although they outnumbered the northerners, the Confederates had a disadvantage—they were attacking a fortified position. Shielded Union soldiers fired upon the Confederates, pinning them behind trees and rocks.

Meanwhile, a Confederate division under General Early had started its attack on the forces holding east Cemetery Hill. The assault was focused on a large brick gate marking the entrance to the cemetery that gave the hill its name. Union artillery had been firing on the southerners all day. The Confederates were eager for revenge—and they got it.

Two Confederate brigades climbed the hill. They fought the Union soldiers in hand-to-hand combat with fists and bayonets, often using their muskets as clubs. Some Confederates reached the top of the hill, but they weren't able to take control of it from the Union troops.

Artist Edwin Forbes, on assignment for Frank Leslie's Illustrated Newspaper, *was a witness to Confederate soldiers charging the cemetery gate.*

As the Confederates waited for reinforcements that never came, Union reinforcements did arrive. With the coming of night—and more Union troops—Early's men were forced to retreat.

As the fighting ended, Ewell's men still held their position halfway up Culp's Hill. They would be ready to renew the attack in the morning. The Confederates hadn't broken the Union line, but they had come close. Lee was determined to strike the crushing blow the next day.

DYING ON A NAMESAKE HILL

John Wesley Culp was born and raised in Gettysburg. In fact, Culp's Hill was named for one of his relatives. As a young man, Culp moved to Virginia to work. When the war broke out, he chose to fight on the side of the Confederacy. In an odd twist of fate, Culp was killed during the fighting on Culp's Hill.

THIRD DAY:

PICKETT'S CHARGE

*U*nion artillery opened fire on General Ewell's men at

dawn. As trees splintered and rocks exploded around them, the

Confederates tried to fight their way up Culp's Hill. They charged

several times, only to be pushed back, leaving piles of dead and

wounded behind. By noon the Confederates were forced to retreat.

Meanwhile, General Lee was finalizing his main plan of attack.

He had tested the Union flanks the day before. Today he would

assault the center. There was only one division—the 6,000 men

under General George Pickett—that hadn't been involved in the

Confederate General Isaac Trimble leads his men in attack.

earlier fighting. They would make up the main attack force. About 6,500 soldiers from General James Pettigrew's and General Isaac Trimble's divisions would join Pickett's division.

LEE'S PLAN

The Confederates formed a line along the eastern slopes of Seminary Ridge. Facing them from behind a stone wall about 1 mile (1.6 km) away was the Union 2nd Corps at Cemetery Ridge. A small group of trees stood in the middle of the Union line.

Once again Longstreet begged Lee to reconsider. He would be sending his men straight at a larger force that was protected by

stone walls and lines of cannons. The number of casualties would be huge. Lee refused. He planned a massive artillery bombardment before the infantry attack. Lee believed the artillery would greatly damage the Union lines and give his men an advantage. Colonel E. Porter Alexander was in charge of placing the 150 cannons that would be used in the attack. He positioned the guns in a giant arc that ran along Seminary Ridge.

DEADLY FIRE

Firing began about 1 p.m. One after the other, the cannons blasted shells at the enemy. But the aim of some cannons was off. Instead of hitting the artillery and infantry at the front of the Union lines, many Confederate shells were landing to the rear of the troops.

The 80-plus Union guns that were lined up on Cemetery Hill quickly responded. Their aim was poor as well. But although their shells were missing the Confederates' artillery, they were landing among the men of Pickett's brigade who were waiting to attack. Even before the battle began, the Confederates were taking heavy casualties.

Then the Union artillery slowed. The hopeful Confederates took this as a sign that the enemy had run out of ammunition. Alexander sent a message to Pickett: "For God's sake come quick!"

Pickett's troops had made it about halfway across the field when the Union artillery again began firing at full strength. Shells burst and cannonballs bounded among the densely packed lines, inflicting heavy casualties. But still the men marched on. Suddenly the left flank came under heavy fire from the 8th Ohio regiment, which had

been posted in front of the Union lines. The Confederates began
rushing toward the center.

The scene repeated as the Confederate right flank came under
deadly artillery fire. As regiments were torn apart, survivors rushed
toward the center of the line. Still they continued their advance.

As the soldiers struggled across the fences that lined Emmitsburg
Road, they faced soldiers from three Pennsylvania regiments. The
Union troops were waiting behind a stone wall that ran along either
side of the trees. As the Confederates pushed their way across the
road, the northerners opened fire.

Thousands of Confederate soldiers were killed or wounded in Pickett's Charge.

Still the Confederates pushed on, firing back and rushing
forward to a spot where the wall formed a 90-degree angle. Only
a few hundred Confederates under General Lewis Armistead
managed to reach the angle. For a moment, it looked as if they
would be victorious. But there were more Union soldiers nearby
to reinforce the wall. All of the surviving Confederates in the angle
were captured. Others near the wall beat a hasty retreat. About
1,100 Confederate soldiers were killed and another 6,000 wounded
or captured in the attack that came to be known as Pickett's Charge.

After the fighting, General Lee rode out to meet his men. "It's all my fault," he told them. "It is I who have lost this fight."

Lee's dreams of crushing the Army of the Potomac and marching on the capital of Washington, D.C., were dead. The battle of Gettysburg had resulted in 28,000 Confederate casualties. Now Lee could only hope to get his troops back to Virginia safely.

ESCAPE TO VIRGINIA

The morning of July 4, Lee kept his army in position just in case Meade ordered a counterattack. Meanwhile, Lee started his 17-mile- (27-km-) long wagon train, piled with wounded men, on the road out of Pennsylvania. He moved the rest of the army under cover of darkness. But Lee need not have worried about the Army of the Potomac. Meade had decided not to press his advantage that day. By the time he was ready to pursue the Confederates, they were already across the Potomac River and headed back to Virginia.

Because the Army of Northern Virginia was allowed to escape Pennsylvania, the Civil War would rage on for two more bloody years. But General Robert E. Lee and his Army of Northern Virginia would never recover from the bitter defeat they suffered at Gettysburg. Immediately after the battle, Lee offered to resign his post as head of the Confederate Army. He had lost confidence in his ability to lead the South to victory.

General Lee's Army of Northern Virginia escapes across the Potomac River.

Confederate President Jefferson Davis refused to accept Lee's resignation. But eventually both men had to accept the fact that the Confederate Army was fighting a war it couldn't win. It had started out with fewer resources and soldiers than the Union, and Gettysburg had taken a staggering toll. On April 9, 1865, General Robert E. Lee would surrender to Union General Ulysses S. Grant, ending the Civil War.

INDEX

Select Bibliography

Catton, Bruce. *Gettysburg: The Final Fury.* Garden City, N.Y.: Doubleday, 1974.

Johnson, Rossiter. *The Fight for the Republic: a Narrative of the More Note-worthy Events in the War of Secession, Presenting the Great Contest in its Dramatic Aspects.* New York: G.P. Putnam's Sons, 1917.

Leehan, Brian. *Pale Horse at Plum Run: The First Minnesota at Gettysburg.* St. Paul: Minnesota Historical Society Press, 2002.

McPherson, James. *Battle Cry of Freedom: The Civil War Era.* New York: Oxford University Press, 2003.

Voices of the Civil War: Gettysburg. Alexandria, Va.: Time-Life Books, 1995.

Ward, Geoffrey C. *The Civil War: An Illustrated History.* New York: Knopf, 1990.

Wheeler, Richard. *Gettysburg 1863: Campaign of Endless Echoes.* New York: Plume, 1999.

Further Reading

Bow, James. *Gettysburg.* New York: Crabtree Pub. Co., 2012.

Martin, Iain C. *Gettysburg: The True Account of Two Young Heroes in the Greatest Battle of the Civil War.* New York: Skyhorse Publishing, Inc., 2013.

Nardo, Don. *Bull Run to Gettysburg: Early Battles of the Civil War.* Mankato, Minn.: Compass Point Books, 2011.

Weber, Jennifer L. *Summer's Bloodiest Days: The Battle of Gettysburg as Told from All Sides.* Washington, D.C.: National Geographic, 2010.

10 a.m.: Union reinforcements under General John Reynolds arrive at McPherson Ridge

1:30 p.m.: Confederate General Robert Rodes' division launches an attack across unscouted territory

2 p.m.: Fighting resumes after a brief lull as Confederate General Richard Ewell's troops arrive

2:10 p.m.: Confederate General Robert E. Lee arrives in Gettysburg

4 p.m.: Confederate General Jubal Early's troops drive the Union's 1st and 11th corps from their position and chase them through town to Cemetery Hill and Culp's Hill

July 2

12:15 a.m.: Union General George Meade arrives in Gettysburg

Early morning: Meade arranges his troops in a defensive line along Cemetery Ridge

1 p.m.: Two-hour artillery duel begins between Union and Confederate guns

Between 2 and 3 p.m.: General George Pickett orders his men to charge the Union lines

July 4

4 p.m.: Confederate General Lewis Armistead and about 200 of his men make it through the Union line, but are defeated; Pickett's charge is a failure

Soldiers and civilians pick up the wounded and bury the dead; General Lee gathers his troops for the retreat back to Virginia

TIMELINE

1863

May 15: Confederate General Robert E. Lee's plan to invade Pennsylvania is approved

June 9: During the Battle of Brandy Station, Confederate General Jeb Stuart's cavalrymen face off against forces under General Alfred Pleasonton

June 25: Stuart leads his cavalry on a prolonged raid against Union troops

June 26: A Confederate scouting party led by General Jubal Early arrives in Gettysburg in search of supplies; General George Meade takes command of the Army of the Potomac

June 30: Union General John Buford leads two cavalry brigades into Gettysburg and sets up a defensive line to the west of town

July 1

7:30 a.m.: Confederate forces clash with Union General Buford's cavalry on the outskirts of Gettysburg

Early afternoon: Union General Daniel Sickles moves his troops out of the Union line

4 p.m.: Confederate General James Longstreet launches the first attack of the day against Sickles' soldiers

4:30 p.m.: General Gouverneur Warren sends for reinforcements for Little Round Top

5:30 p.m.: The 20th Maine repels a Confederate attack to hold Little Round Top

8 p.m.: Fighting across Cemetery Hill and Culp's Hill intensifies

Midnight: Confederates retreat to the middle of Culp's Hill

July 3

4 a.m.: Union artillery begins firing on Confederate forces encamped on Culp's Hill

INTERNET SITES

Use FactHound to find Internet sites related to this book. All of the sites on FactHound have been researched by our staff.

Here's all you do:
Visit *www.facthound.com*
Type in this code: 9780756546953

GLOSSARY

ARTILLERY—large, powerful guns, such as cannons

BATTALION—military unit consisting of headquarters and two or more companies; a company consists of 80 to 250 soldiers

BAYONET—sharp blade attached to the end of a musket or rifle

BRIGADE—unit of an army consisting of two or more regiments

CASUALTY—someone who is wounded, captured, killed, or missing in a war

CAVALRY—unit of soldiers who fight on horseback

CORPS—large military unit consisting of two to five divisions

DEPLOY—place in battle formation

DIVISION—military unit consisting of several brigades

FLANK—the right or left of a military formation

FORTIFY—make stronger against an attack

GARRISON—a group of soldiers based in a town and ready to defend it

INFANTRY—soldiers who fight on foot

MILITIA—citizens who volunteer to serve as soldiers during emergencies

ORDERLY—soldier assigned to perform tasks for a superior officer

PIKE—road; short for turnpike

REGIMENT—military unit consisting of two or more battalions